between the apple and the bite

between the apple and the bite

poems about women's predicaments
in history and mythology

Sue Woodward

Publication © Modjaji Books 2021
Text © Sue Woodward 2021
First published in 2021 by Modjaji Books Pty Ltd
www.modjajibooks.co.za

ISBN 978-1-928433-23-1

Editor: Arja Salafranca
Cover artist: Hazel Woodward
https://hazeljeanwoodward.wixsite.com/hazelspaintings
Book design and layout: Liz Gowans

Set in Adobe Garamond Pro and Acumin Variable Concept

The poems in *between the apple and the bite* are concerned with the choices, predicaments and celebrations of women in mythology, history and in contemporary times. Women take responsibility for much that goes wrong in gender interactions, including their own responses to disrespect and abuse. In these poems I put myself in the place of women such as Helen of Troy and Joan of Arc and imagine their responses to their predicaments.

I include notes as background to the stories for those readers unfamiliar with them. The poems reflect only fragments of the women's lives; the notes are an attempt to fill in some background for a better understanding of their place in Western culture and history.

Contents

I

II

III

space and time collide
in light on ramses' face
the planets conjoin
pandora opens the box
and judas kisses the cheek

paradise is lost
in the blink of a serpent's gaze
between the apple and the bite
and the spark and the beginning
the forest burns

I

eve

in our favourite spot, in the embrace
of god's tree, the last rays of the sun
are blocked by solid granite, the rocks
dark humped monsters crouch heavy

the wind shivers the poplar leaves, silver
maracas harmonising with distant barks
calling adolescent baboons to bed
we sit lonely and companionable

you are content with mapping the stars
as they appear in tiny pricks and patterns
sirius, orion, canopus, the dog

I chat, keep my hands busy ask questions
what if and why, why the stars why the fruit
why the moment of freedom between the apple

and the bite, why am I wholly woman when I
contemplate the abyss, when I hold forbidden
fruit sink my teeth into waxen skin
bite off a chunk of flesh?

eve

The selection for 'predicaments' starts and ends with poems about Eve's predicament at being blamed for tempting Adam into sin by offering him the forbidden fruit. Centuries of misogyny have arisen over Eve's responsibility for this original sin. Initially I thought to explore the Genesis story of Adam and Eve as an example of the fleeting moment in time between an idea and an action, the apple being the idea and the bite being the action – the moment of pure freedom before the consequences set in. The poem took on a life of its own and became an account of Eve's predicament as a consequence of making the choice between innocence and experience.

Source: Genesis 2.15 – 3.24

leda

arriving in good time not believing my luck if i could get this part it would be the break of a lifetime a sidekick leads me over thick grass to a river bank with an umbrella a lounger champagne in an ice bucket one glass he fills the glass i settle on the lounger sip on popping bubbles in dry heat like the karoo in a drought my body under an electric blanket my cheeks flushed with the champagne heat prickles of sweat dotting my neck i sip watch the condensation on the bucket drip onto the grass he fills the glass i wait i sip the air rising in vertical hazy waves i am melting into the lounger the lounger creaks a heavier weight covers my body a feather boa around my neck feathers brushing my cheek my ear nibbled i can't breathe can't move with the weight my arms pinioned a stink of slime and underwater murk a bass drum beating on my chest in my chest a small tapping to get out my breaths shallow so faint they stop before i die they kick start i am breathing the heaviness slides to one side the weight is gone the sidekick appears *we'll let you know* and shows me out

leda

Many writers of Greek mythology have told the story of Zeus' rape of Leda. Zeus desired the beautiful Leda, and in order to seduce her changed himself into a swan, and pretended to be escaping from a bird of prey. After the rape, Leda slept with her own husband, Tyndareus, the King of Sparta. The two encounters resulted in two fertilised eggs, each with a set of twins, Helen (of Troy) and Pollux, and Castor and Clytemnestra. I have given the scene of the rape a contemporary setting based on allegations from within the #metoo movement.

Source: https://www.greeklegendsandmyths.com/leda.html

pandora

I am a gift bearing a gift
a sealed jar, a punishment
a punishment for an outrage
an outrage at a brazen theft of fire
a fire for heat, a lucifer for light
a torch for protection, glowing
coals for holding back the night

I am a woman to be trusted
with such a gift, or why the gift
a woman chosen for her strength
or why be chosen
the jar, heavy, engraved
the seal easily broken
a meeting of eyes
a threshold crossed
the jar opened
the punishment
released
an infinite stream
of inhumanity greed
and dominion

in the dregs
hope
or the illusion of hope

pandora

Like Eve in the Biblical story, Pandora in Greek mythology was the first human woman, created on the instructions of Zeus, in order to get even with Prometheus, who had tricked the gods. Prometheus later tricked the gods again by stealing fire from them to give to humanity. Pandora, created from clay and water, was endowed with several gifts from the gods, one of which was curiosity, and was herself given as a gift to Epimetheus, the half-brother of Prometheus. The jar, a gift from Zeus, contained all the evils of the world, as well as an enduring glimmer of hope for human beings.

Source: https://www.greeklegendsandmyths.com/pandora.html

echo

i stand by with your towel
as they do at the tennis
you take it, roughly
rub your glistening skin
and dripping hair
you toss the towel
i stoop to pick it up
hold it to my cheek
breathe deeply
of your sweat

at the mirror
you flex your biceps
this way, that way
change your stance
lock your fingers
lats pecs traps
i know them all
i stand behind you
a wraith at your shoulder
you notice me 'buff huh?'
'buff' i say

echo

The nymph Echo was cursed by the goddess Hera so that she no longer had a voice of her own; she could only repeat the words of others. She fell in love with the handsome Narcissus, who had many admirers, both male and female. Because of the curse Echo could only follow Narcissus, waiting for him to speak so that she could repeat his words. When he rejected her she hid herself in a cave, not eating or sleeping until she withered away. All that was left of her was her voice. The goddess Nemesis decided to punish Narcissus for not accepting Echo's love, and caused him to fall in love with his own reflection in a deep pool. Narcissus refused to leave the beautiful boy he saw in the pool, and he too died of pining and starvation. His final words were: "Farewell dear boy, beloved in vain", which Echo picked up and repeated.
Source: https://www.greeklegendsandmyths.com/echo-and-narcissus.html

circe

he had followed his men from the beach
and now stood before me, late sunlight
caressing his flanks, a sea stallion
fine spray of brine on his beard

nostrils flaring he asked what I had done
to his men, brothers all, their mothers' sons
made in the image of their fathers, formed
as warriors of winds and wars and whores

I told him I had transformed them
he asked why, I said because they are pigs
he asked, why are they pigs, I said
because I transformed them

I and their mothers transformed them
as they toddled from their cradles
took up sticks, smacked their sisters
spat and cursed at their mothers

I showed him the pens, downwind, side by side
a boar in each, hairy hams touching concrete slabs
legs astride a gutter choked with bodily excretions
snouts permanently in the trough

continued

he demanded I return them to themselves
lunged at me, I fell at his feet, hugged his legs
begged him to come to my bed, hold me
give me sons to form and transform

circe
Circe was the daughter of Helios the sun god, which meant that she was a goddess and immortal.
Because she defied the gods, she was banished to the island of Aeaea to live out her eternity alone. On
this wild island she perfected her knowledge of herbs and magic, and was able to transform people into
animals. On his return journey from Troy, Odysseus landed on Aeaea with his men, who were rough and
badly behaved. Circe turned them into pigs. In this poem I have imagined consequences for them in the
context of modern women's increasing anger at men's disrespect, abuse and violence. Circe however, is
conflicted and lonely and needs to perpetuate the cycle of life by taking Odysseus as her lover.
Source: https://www.greeklegendsandmyths.com/circe.html

eurydice

your strides too long i content myself
with two steps for one, keep my eyes
on the backs of your legs, your calves
tense and relax as you walk

the hours consume miles of dark terrain
your bronzed muscles more intimate
to me than my own pallid flesh which falters
from lack of use in my subterranean prison

we make steady progress to a stream
your sandals cleave the water like boats
on an open sea, my feet slip on mossy rocks
i bite my hand for fear of crying out

wet slippers are no protection against sharp
stones, sand gives way, scree is treacherous
you leap a small chasm i hesitate on the edge
and watch as the gap between us widens

your dear frame silhouetted against the dawn
i whisper your name, my voice faint as your fingers
brushing a single string of your lyre, you stop, turn
i miss my footing, cry out, slip into the chasm

eurydice

Orpheus had an extraordinary musical talent, and gods, humans, beasts and even the rocks and trees would move to hear him singing and playing his lyre. Orpheus fell in love with Eurydice, and she with him. They were married and lived happily, until Eurydice accidently disturbed a nest of vipers, was bitten and died instantly. Orpheus was inconsolable and decided to go to the underworld to plead with Hades to allow Eurydice to return to the earth. Armed with his exquisite voice and his lyre, Orpheus so charmed Hades, Persephone, and Cerberus, the three-headed dog of the underworld, that Hades agreed to let Eurydice return home with Orpheus. The only condition was that Orpheus should not look back until Eurydice was out in the light. If he did Eurydice would be taken back to the underworld, never to return. Sadly, Orpheus looked back and lost Eurydice forever.

Source: https://www.greeklegendsandmyths.com/eurydice.html

helen

In the evening the women are permitted to stand on the battlements to watch the culmination of the day's battle. The sun is setting in a stain of red. Our men are marching raggedly through the gates of Troy, Hector in front, then Paris, Glaucus and the others.

The Greeks have retreated to their ships, their wagons loaded with dead bodies and a scrapheap of shields, helmets and spears. Tomorrow will be the same. There is a cold wind. The king leaves to greet the returning soldiers. A brazier is burning, the guards are at ease.

I have an impulse to grab a sword, thrust its metal shaft into the brazier, hold it until it burns crimson, press it to my cheeks, set my hair to burning, blister my brows, sear my lips, cauterise my ears. My face would run like lava, turn a thousand wooden ships to stone.

helen

The story of Helen of Troy is told by Homer in his epic poem, the *Iliad*. Helen was a child of the god Zeus and Leda, who was raped by Zeus in the guise of a swan. Helen grew to be exquisitely beautiful and married Menelaus, the king of Sparta. The goddess Aphrodite promised the Trojan prince, Paris, that if he, as judge, selected Aphrodite as the winner of a beauty competition with Athena and Hera, she would give him Helen in exchange. Paris did as he was asked and judged Aphrodite the most beautiful of the three goddesses. Then he travelled to the court of Menelaus, seduced Helen and fled with her to his ship. Menelaus called on all the Greek kings to avenge his honour, and with his brother Agamemnon, and the heroes Odysseus and Achilles, built up a force of a thousand ships to wage war on the Trojans. The war lasted for ten years and ended with the deaths of dozens of Greek and Trojan heroes, including Hector, Achilles and Paris. The Elizabethan playwright, Christopher Marlowe, penned the famous lines about Helen in his play, Doctor Faustus, "Was this the face that launched a thousand ships, and burnt the topless towers of Ilium?"

Source: https://www.ancient-origins.net/myths-legends/helen-troy-beauty-sparked-trojan-war-002076

cassandra

in the laundry
ironing
his shirt
a reverie
of crisp mathematics
left side, right side, collar, cuff
puff puff of a miniature steam train
i am assaulted by a cold front of brut
nuzzling my neck
twisted bent backwards
to face jowls
zooming in like a macro lens
ironing board
pressing into my spine
wet mulberry lips
hot mussel of tongue
a blind sea creature finding its way
i run from the reek of scorching cotton
an iron shaped brand
on a versace shirt
a dismissal for lying

cassandra

There are several versions of Cassandra's story in Greek mythology. Cassandra was a daughter of King Priam of Troy and Queen Hecuba. She was granted the gift of prophecy by the god Apollo, but when she rejected his sexual advances, he punished her by leaving her with the gift but with the curse that no one would believe her. Cassandra is said to have foretold the fall of Troy and warned against bringing the wooden horse into the gates of Troy. She was not believed and considered to be a madwoman.

Source: https://www.britannica.com/topic/Cassandra-Greek-mythology

penelope

from behind the hills the dawn arrives
   in a splash of light
setting the drapes on fire and where they fail
to close a shaft of gold on the opposite wall
i slip from the covers
open the curtains widen the gap flood
the room with unrestrained sunlight
i look to the line of horizon –
the turquoise of the ionian
the cerulean of the sky
no sail on the unwavering blue

i regard my image in the polished surface
   of my mirror
what will you see when you return
features sharper, eyes deeper pools
small creases at the corners
mouth harder from disuse and resolve
hair still lustrous, breasts heavier
more exciting perhaps, an older woman
after twenty years working and reworking
this old tapestry, what can i say to match
your world, your world beyond this dawn

penelope

Penelope was the wife of Odysseus, also known as Ulysses. The Greek epic poet Homer tells the story of Odysseus' 20 year long travels and adventures. All this time Penelope waited at home on the island of Ithaca for him to return to her and their son Telemachus.
Source: https://www.greeklegendsandmyths.com/penelope.html

II

delilah

I have you this time
no more teasing
with ropes and riddles
your head
is heavy in my lap
my song a lullaby
from a land beyond
the lake, my fingers
a comb to smooth
your tangled mane
black as night, shot
through with trails
of silver, your pelt
the soft sand
of the desert at dawn

your eyelids flutter
your breathing
steadies, I signal
for the maid to bring
the blades
she does not understand
my love-hate
stroking of your curls
this need for power

continued

I am chosen for this
the chosen have no choice
careful not to tug
I hack
you do not wake

delilah

The story of Samson and Delilah comes from the Old Testament. Samson had enormous strength. As a young man, he killed a lion with his bare hands. He fell in love with Delilah, whom the Philistines bribed to tell them the secret of Samson's strength. Delilah pleaded with Samson to tell her his secret, but Samson gave her false ways to contain him, such as tying him up with his own locks. Delilah tried all of his remedies but none of them worked, and eventually he gave in and told her the secret – "If I be shaven then my strength will go from me, and I shall become weak and be like any other man". *Source: Judges 16*

salome

I am to choose a reward
for my dancing, I think
of perfume, gold bangles
to my elbow, a mud bath
from jordan, dragon robe
of silk, a falcon, a lute,
an ivory fan…

mama has a different idea
she whispers in my ear
her words drop like stones
to my belly, she forgets
that when a gecko falls
I pick it up, carry its
translucent body carefully
to the courtyard, watch it climb
hand over hand to the safety
of the jasmine…

now I am chosen to bear
a heavier weight…
a man's head on a silver plate
a reward for my dancing

salome

Salome was the daughter of Herodias and the stepdaughter of Herod Antipas. John the Baptist angered Herodias by disapproving of her marriage to Herod. Herod imprisoned John the Baptist but was afraid to execute him, which Herodias wanted him to do, because John the Baptist was popular with the people. When Salome pleased Herod by her dancing, he promised her anything she wanted, and prompted by her mother, she asked for the head of John the Baptist.
Source: Matthew 14.1 – 14.12

judith

the powers of my sex
an angle of chin, a toss
of hair, an imperceptible
swing of the hips, a flash
of flesh, a widening of eyes
are an insult to me

you are a fool to fall
for these things and not
the complexities of my mind
my gift for language
joy at a shaft of sunlight
penetrating to the depths
of the forest

I am not a woman desperate
for the rasp of a man's beard
on my cheek, I grip
the sword, give the nod
the servant holds your head
I close my eyes
strike with both hands
surprisingly
it is done

judith
The Book of Judith is in the Apochrypha. It tells the story of the beautiful widow, Judith, who, accompanied by a servant, bravely gains entry into the enemy camp of Holofernes, an Assyrian invading general, to seduce and kill him. She gains his trust, and one night when he is drunk, she decapitates him and takes his head back to her countrymen. The invading Assyrians, having lost their leader, disperse, and Judith's people, the Israelites, are freed from oppression.
Source: en.wikipedia.org/wiki/Book-of-Judith/

mary then

at fourteen, with limited options
I was betrothed, after the vision
my belly swelled, I expected
a beating, the old man said only
we must go from here

the confinement was less than adequate
the packing up, fleeing, hiding, an ordeal
much later when I lost my son
I understood my body was a vehicle
my discomforts irrelevant

mary now

my eggs extracted and frozen
they nestle in liquid nitrogen
in a sterile facility

at the optimal time
I will select sperm
donor unknown
for race, intelligence, gender
and start the procedure

it will be an immaculate conception
a caesarean birth
I will be a virgin mother

mary then and mary now
Mary, the mother of Jesus, has played a huge role in the history of Christianity. I have not sought to diminish her role, but rather to understand her situation as a young wife and mother, and as a woman in a modern context.
Source: Luke 1:26 – 1.38

mary of magdala

the band of twelve, and me, formed the core group
joined from time to time by itinerants and wannabes
our feet blistered calf muscles aching we walked
miles between villages along goat tracks over passes
they needed me for my networking I needed them
for their banter their loyalty camaraderie protection
we all needed him, our leader

we knew one of us was chosen to be the betrayer
we did not know it would be by that most intimate
of gestures, the soft footfall, the hand on the shoulder
the gentle brushing of cracked lips on a sunburnt cheek
it wasn't me – my predicament came later, my part
rewritten, chosen as the counterbalance, the whore
the representative of my gender

mary of magdala

Mary Magdalene was first mentioned in the Gospel of Luke as one of the women who travelled with Jesus and his disciples, and was a witness to the crucifixion, burial and resurrection of Jesus. In 581 AD Pope Gregory 1, in a series of sermons conflated Mary Magdalene with an unnamed 'sinful woman', which resulted in the widespread and inaccurate belief that she was a repentant prostitute. In 1969 Pope Paul VI removed this identification but the perception persisted in popular culture.

Source: smithsonianmag.com/history/who-was-mary-magdalene-119565482

the other mary

i was there that day
in the background
as always, reserved
knowing the answer
saying it softly, not heard
above the keening
of the marys, not asked
for my role in the drama
my carrying of the oils
the sweet-smelling spices
the shoving at the rock
kicking aside the crumpled
sheet, blinded by the light
dropping to the dust
weeping
for a missing dead man
praying
for myself
the other mary

the other mary

In the New Testament three Marys are mentioned to have been present at Jesus' crucifixion and resurrection. There has been debate as to which Mary was being referred to as 'the other Mary' at the tomb. To quote from Matthew 27:61: "And there was Mary Magdalene, and the other Mary, sitting over against the sepulchre."
Source: Matthew 27:61

the girl who created the milky way

when i become a woman
my mother hides me in a small hut
my brothers track, hunt, eat meat, dance
my food is tubers, baking in ash
not to be eaten until the men return

a flame of anger rises to my cheeks
my teeth clash like a trapped jackal's
my nails dig into my flesh
i creep into the night
the stars are distant, the moon
a sliver of translucent shell

i bend down, scoop warm woodash
into my hands and roasted roots
i toss them with all my strength
flinging my arms wide
across the arc of the sky
the ashes fly high
from sunset to sunrise
lighting up the night
the red and white roots stars
in the silver stream of spilt milk

i have lit the sky with my fire
made a path for my brothers
to find their way home

---

the girl who created the milky way

The Khoisan people had numerous myths and stories to explain their natural environment. One of these is the story of the creation of the Milky Way. Marguerite Poland used this rich oral folklore tradition in her children's stories in the award-winning books *Mantis and the Moon* and *The Woodash Stars*, on which I have based this poem.

jeanne

my inquisitors' questions jab like the beaks of crows prying
for an eye socket, piercing a wrist, stabbing at a naked throat
I am steadfast in my answers, if they would analyse the whole
they would know that truth is unwavering, if I lied I would
    forget
what I answered previously over the weary days of my trial

'Why do you cause yourself to be adored?'
'Are you in God's grace?'
'What do the voices tell you?'
'Why do you wear men's clothes?'
'Why do you dance in the moonlight beneath the ancient oak
    of Bourlement?'

'I can only answer to you the truth that I know, the rest I
    deny...'

the truth that I know is the bedrock
after layers of soil are worn away
it is the frost beneath bare feet
stars flung against a velvet sky
blood trickling from slowly opened flesh
it is the fire
the licking tongues of dragons
the open jaws of caves of infernal heat
it is the fire that burns the forest to ash
the flames sucking at my feet

continued

it is death and salvation
it is the fire
oh the fire, I fear the fire
I fear it

jeanne

Joan of Arc was born in 1412 in a small village in France. She had a close relationship with God, which included hearing voices of angels. The voices told her to drive the English out of France, and to conduct the Dauphin Charles to Reims to be crowned King of France. At the age of nineteen she built up a small army, which she led into battle against the English. She freed the city of Orleans and drove the English out of the Loire valley, finally conducting Charles to his coronation. The English wanted to discredit Charles as a false king and imprisoned Joan. Together with the Church authorities, an English court condemned Joan as a heretic and a witch. Her trial began in February 1431 and on 30 May of that year she was convicted and burned at the stake. Twenty-five years later the findings against her were declared null and void and in 1920 she was canonised a saint. The complete transcripts of her trial still exist and are available on the internet.

Source: www.stjoan-center.com/Trials/sec14.html

saartjie

their promises drop
from thin lips like bokdrolle*
from a klipspringer's anus

after london they sell me
to paris for 'research'
i stand or sit, legs apart,
with other children of africa
a baby rhino, a fur-patched
baboon, a crocodile in a filthy
puddle of wet

the spectators poke with sticks
and umbrellas, we retreat
to our corners, to our memories
of sky and red ochre earth

*Bokdrolle: small pellets of buck dung

saartjie

Sara Baartman, a Khoikhoi woman, was born around 1789 in the Eastern Cape. By the age of sixteen Sara had lost both her parents and her husband, and with the expansion of Dutch colonialism, was sold into slavery to become a domestic servant in Cape Town. In 1810 she 'signed' a contract to be taken to England to work as a domestic servant and to be exhibited for entertainment purposes. With her unusual colouring and body shape, Sara was put on display in a cage with exhibits of people displaying physical oddities or deformities. Four years later Sara was sold to a man in France who showcased animals. Eventually in 1815 she was taken over by a naturalist, who used her for anatomical research. In 1816, at the age of only twenty-six, Sara died of alcoholism in Paris. In 2002 Sara Baartman's remains were returned to South Africa by the French Government, and were buried at Hankey in the Eastern Cape.

Source: https://www.sahistory.org.za/people/sara-saartjie-baartman

marie antoinette

today my cappuccino has the image
of an ear of wheat nestling on dense foam
my husband has a thin white moustache
he tells me he heard from someone who
knows someone in the city that the people
are dying, i ask why, he says it is because
they have no food, i am puzzled, if they
are dying why are they walking
on the highways pushing trolleys piled
high like migrating beetles, I am shocked
at another instance of fake news

later we stand on our balcony in a black
southeaster, my hair whips across my eyes
the wind stops my ears, my husband pulls
my wrap around my shoulders, the people
are dancing in the street singing waving
sticks, i wonder at the cause of such frivolity
on a bitter winter's night, they look up, see us
bend down, pick up bricks and bottles
hurl them, their mouths distorted
eyes fingerholes in old grey dough

marie antoinette

Marie Antoinette became Queen of France at the age of nineteen when her young husband Louis XVI
became king. Louis was a weak king and Marie Antoinette became embroiled in political and social
intrigues. She lived a fabulously extravagant lifestyle and was seen by the people as a symbol of the
excesses of the monarchy. In 1789, after the wheat crops failed, and the consequent high prices for bread
brought widespread hunger to the already desperately poor peasantry, workers and peasants stormed the
Bastille Prison and began the French Revolution. Three years later the monarchy was abolished and the
following year Louis was tried, convicted of treason, and by order of the revolutionary tribunal, condemned
to death by guillotine. Marie Antoinette was condemned to her own death a few months later.

Source: https://www.history.com/topics/france/marie-antoinette

mata hari

I am ready
unbound unblinded
twelve boys in khaki and kepis
line up, rifles at ease
I am close enough
at fifteen paces
to see the glisten of down
on an upper lip
to smell fear in their sweat
I stand tall
framed in my gainsborough hat
black velvet and ermine
silk ribbons louis heels
I played you at your own game
you changed the rules
I, dancer mother lover negotiator
am ready

mata hari

Mata Hari, born Margaretha Zelle in 1876 to Dutch parents, was beautiful, precocious, clever and spoilt. By the time she was eighteen Margaretha's father had abandoned the family and her mother had died. Margaretha moved to The Hague, answered an advertisement for 'a girl of pleasant character', and married Captain Rudolf MacLeod, an official of the Dutch East India Company based in Indonesia. Captain MacLeod turned out to be a serial philanderer and a wife beater. After contracting syphilis from him and bearing two children, both of whom died young, she was soon divorced and in need of supporting herself. She re-invented herself as Mata Hari, an exotic dancer, who interpreted 'the temple dances of the Indies'. Her dancing was sensuous and erotic, if scandalous for the time, and Mata Hari became wildly popular all over Europe. Much in demand as a courtesan and enjoying the company of rich and powerful men, she travelled widely and spoke a number of languages. Evidence for her recruitment and actual activity as a spy for Germany and France during World War I is thin and has been cast into doubt in later years. Suspected and interrogated by the English, and set up as a German spy by the French, she was arrested in February 1917. In July she was tried and sentenced to be executed by firing squad. Later the prosecutor confessed that there was 'not enough evidence in the case to flog a cat'. Her execution was carried out in great secrecy in the early morning of 15 October 1917.
Source: en.wikipedia.org/wiki/Mata_Hari

III

adamastor wakes

"Even as I spoke, an immense shape
Materialised in the night air,
Grotesque and of enormous stature,
With heavy jowls, and an unkempt beard,
Scowling from shrunken, hollow eyes,
Its complexion earthy and pale,
Its hair grizzled and matted with clay,
Its mouth coal black, teeth yellow with decay."

From Luis de Camoes, The Luciads (1)

it is uncertain what woke him
the traffic was bad that night
and the people partied on
ringing lampposts like chimes
shattering bottles
in wild percussion

the bitch knew alright
she strained at her chains
and hurled herself at the gate
flesh and steel clashing
in a mess of blood and foam

the foghorn moaned
a soft rain fell
but what woke him is uncertain
it could have been the dawn

adamastor wakes

The quoted lines are from *The Luciads (1)* (published in 1572) by the Portuguese epic poet, Luis de Camoes.
In *The Luciads (1)* Camoes describes Vasco da Gama's perilous journey around the Cape of Storms, during
which he and his crew encounter a terrifying vision of the giant Adamastor, who upbraids them for
trespassing on his territory and foretells their doom.
Source: https://en.wikipedia.org/wiki/Adamastor

butterfly

in the beginning
the dome you built
was ample, our wings
filled the vast space
with their symmetrical beating
you showed me how to soar
until i was giddy
with dancing spinning sinking
resting
beside your pond

i did not notice
your quicksilver diving
your disappearing
reappearing, streaming
bright water
i listened
for the sound of your wings
mine becoming quiet
diminishing

now i no longer smear the glass
with the mucus of my longing
my shrivelled wings are folded
waiting for your return

a possibility of poignancy

when the days merge one
with the other in an eternity
of waiting, for something
anything, a call a text a 'like'
an accident or god be thanked
a poignant moment

take me behind the dunes
and hold me in the moment
for now and for a short time after
feed me on glances in passing
a locking of eyes, a brushing of fingers
a possibility of poignancy

silence of the girls

cannot will not must not
my tongue is rooted in ice
eyes scrubbed with salt
ears stopped skull shaved
torso bound in bubble wrap
dead woman's fingers
white sausages
on concrete slab
wet shoulder-blades
cleaning slicing
trimming chopping
vacuum-packed
stacked
stored
at -5°
must not
may not
will not

divine right

at night images tumble
about my head like packs
of cards, slipping through my fingers
as I grasp for a king, a jack or even
a joker from the hot stream of general
anxiety, needing to be in the game
in the thrall of acceptance, sexuality
verbal dexterity, foreplay, the art
of lunge and riposte, handicapped
by the ancient rule of the father
tangled in a confusion of lessons
passed from mother to daughter:
the desire to be desired
never to give offence
the divine right of kings

truth

one afternoon at grandma's house
I wondered: 'if truth is a thread in
this lace cloth should I follow the thread
and become lost in stitches and loops
and patterns, or should I embrace the whole
and stumble under the weight of illusion?'

now the cloth is mine and I love
the weight and texture of it on my table
an intricate mandala of matriarchs
girlfriends, daughters, mothers of sons lost
to gangs and guns and water and wine
interwoven patterns of truth

running with the moon

we ran with the moon along an unfolding shore of silver
no start to the race, or finish, unknown to each other
we ran to beat the tide, to drown in a quicksilver sea
to meet our shadows in naked radiance
wheeling like gulls, smooth as seals, flying like fish

we ran between two rivers, salt sucking at our footprints
feet scattering coins of water drops, bright as tears
old as pieces of eight, young as bitcoin

at the fast-moving ribbon of river, we pulled up, rearing
milling like white horses, until at an unspoken word
we retraced our steps

moonwashed
ghost crabs at low tide

an act of violence

it began calmly enough
a thought, a sentence
an insult that became a tide
feeding upon itself and
drawing on deeply buried sources
it picked me up
and bowled me along
in an intensity of anger
foul words came
haltingly at first
quickly gained confidence
and spilled onto the page
black ink on ivory bond
a signature forced self control
i sealed the missive
and delivered it
by hand

the swimming pool

david hockney –
i am lying at the bottom of your pool
opaque in translucence
curving acutely
a poem out of kilter

i will go soon
there are problems of breathing
and besides it is your pool
but for now i shall lie here
and think about my part in this
as my limbs dissolve
there are no ripples
only patterns of light
dispersing and merging

i am one
i am the poet and the poem
i return
water in water
luminous in light
at the door you indicate that the poem
should not leave the premises
i comply and step into the sun

the swimming pool

The twentieth-century artist David Hockney was born and grew up under grey skies in the rainy city of Manchester in the United Kingdom. When he first visited California in the United States he was struck by the sunlight, the blue skies and the abundance of water, particularly water in suburban swimming pools and showers. He made a series of huge murals, as well as many smaller paintings, of light reflected on water in swimming pools.

I thought it was you

I thought it was you
at the Golden Acre
where the beggar flaunts his torso
and the children their innocence

I thought it was you
on the Grand Parade
where sharp men play the glass bead game
with country boys in hats

I thought it was you
on the beach at Sunrise
where the spent and the misspent
take communion in the ocean

I thought it was you
on the train at Mowbray
though my eyes were tired
from the glare of dark men

and you, did you think it was me
on an underground somewhere
moving fast in a press of shoulders
surging towards the light?

farewell my friend

I wanted to talk to you
about the tibetan book,
conscious dying, going
softly into the night,
but you were the star
of your own show
smoking medicinal marijuana
laughing through the pain

and when at last the visitors
were gone, and the glasses
and cups were washed
there were no more words
you lay in your nest
a baby bird unfeathered
a heap of angles
sleeping your life away

requiem for my father

we sit straight-backed
soft in light dandling dust
through stained glass
silent as your footsteps
on the granite

you in your suit lie dark
straightjacketed still as stone
and the silence
of your footstep
is an ocean in our ears

"*The rain fell between them like a curtain of splintered glass.*"
– Truman Capote

between the apple and the bite

beneath god's tree lived a man and a woman
the man-made patterns of the stars
the woman spoke with snakes
one day at dusk the sun was sinking
and the full moon rising, the woman
climbed the tree and picked god's perfect
sphere of green, she held it between her palms
and knew the power of the idea

am i, should i, do i
yes said the snake
yes said the man
and god watched
as she bit a chunk
of pure white flesh

spit it out said god
it wasn't me said the man
spit it out said god
it wasn't me said the snake
spit it out said god
it wasn't me said the woman

god watched
as the man
took hold of the woman
held her down
she spat and spat
with dry mouth
and swollen tongue
until the crisp fruit
plopped into his hand
the man let it fall

crushing it beneath
his sole

and knew the power
of love and rage
in his arms

he held the woman
licked her face
the seeds grew
the woman tended them
through sun and rain
the man built a cage of thorns
captured the serpent
milked its venom

and knew the power
of life and death
in his hands

god watched
as the woman
felt the sting of his hand on her face
and the weight of life in her belly
she hoisted his load on her shoulders
and knew the consequences
of choice

Acknowledgements

With thanks to the following:

New Contrast:
the swimming pool, requiem for my father (as 'at your requiem'), quote from my poem 'exquisite', farewell my friend, the girl who created the milky way (as 'becoming')

Litnet new writing:
I thought it was you (25 November 2016)

New Coin:
eve, judith, leda, mary (as 'mary then and now')

McGregor Poetry Festival Anthology 2019:
running with the moon (first prize Mc Gregor Poetry Competition 2019), judith, inheritance

Sol Plaatjie EU Anthology 2014:
adamastor wakes

I would like to thank Robert Berold for his guidance and encouragement, Derek Thomas for initial layout and design, Hazel Woodward for permission to use her beautiful painting on the cover, Wendy Woodward for kind and positive mentoring, Peter and Alice Wilkes, Rob and my wonderful family and friends for their support.

About the author

Sue Woodward has spent most of her life in Cape Town although she was born and educated in Johannesburg. She studied English and Psychology at the University of the Witwatersrand, became a teacher and then a writer and editor of educational materials and children's stories. She has been published in many journals and anthologies and in 2019 won the McGregor Poetry Festival competition. *between the apple and the bite* is her debut collection of poetry. She lives in Muizenberg close to the sea, the mountains and the vlei.

"In these poems Sue Woodward works in a mode of some of the most powerful contemporary poems in English: Deryn Rees-Jones, Fiona Benson and Alice Oswald have recent collections in which Homeric figures are foregrounded. The poems in Woodward's collection also have Biblical bases; in a re-imagining and re-contextualisation of old "western" myths we are given new insights into how the old tropes are present in our own psyches."
                                                        – Joan Metelerkamp

Printed in the United States
by Baker & Taylor Publisher Services